YOUR YEAR OF WONDERS

YOUR
YEAR OF
WONDERS

EMBRACE CHANGE
GROW FASTER
WIN BIGGER

NICK TASLER

Edited by Wendy Weckwerth

ISBN 13: 978-1-64343-546-6
Library of Congress Catalog Number: 2024937480
Printed in the United States of America
First Printing: 2025
29 28 27 26 25   5 4 3

Cover design by Chainbot Solutions
Interior design by Pat Maloney

 Beaver's Pond Press, Inc.
939 Seventh Street West
Saint Paul, Minnesota 55102
(952) 829-8818
www.BeaversPondPress.com

To order, visit www.ItascaBooks.com
or call (800) 901-3480. Reseller discounts available.

CONTENTS

CHAPTER ONE

THE WINNER'S DILEMMA

Winning takes talent, to repeat takes character.
—John Wooden

A few years ago, a junior partner at a successful financial services firm saw me speak and asked me if I could help him out of a rut. Javier had come from relatively humble beginnings in a working-class neighborhood. After excelling at a public university, he secured an uncommon invitation to join the Wall Street world of Ivy League investment bankers. Fast-forward a decade and a half. Not yet forty years old, he'd surpassed his lifetime net worth goal *many* times over. He had two healthy kids, had a happy marriage, and had already accomplished more in the realm of philanthropy than most executives twenty years his senior.

To me, Javier looked like the embodiment of the American Dream. But he felt stuck. He wasn't sleeping well. He wasn't in the physical shape he wanted to be in. He was questioning his judgment.

My first thought? *This is all in his head.* That's what I

expected to find when I interviewed his team members. I imagined these interviews going something like the final scene in *It's a Wonderful Life* when George Bailey's friends and neighbors all come together to show the downtrodden George just how swell he really is.

To my surprise, rather than refuting Javier's doubts, the interviewees confirmed them. Javier's direct reports tactfully told me that his incredible talents were not being maximized because he was holding on too tightly to lower-level projects and responsibilities that he could easily hand over to them. Javier had already mentioned difficulty delegating, so that wasn't a total surprise.

But it wasn't until my interview with Javier's boss that the full picture snapped into focus. The senior partner, a guy with a sailor's zeal for expletive-laden diatribes, made it clear that Javier had stopped thinking like a rainmaker and started thinking like a bean counter. Javier was working longer hours than ever before, but only on low-risk projects that would—at best—add up to minor incremental improvements. He was trying to cut expenses when he was supposed to be swinging for the fences.

PING-PONG PARADOX

A while back, I used to work at this little start-up. Like all self-respecting start-ups, we had a Ping-Pong table. A few of us in the office thought we were pretty good at Ping-Pong since we'd occasionally whupped the neighbor kids in our basements while growing up.

But our lead software engineer, Yufan Chen, was on

another level. While growing up in Taiwan, Yufan had played on a competitive table tennis team with uniforms and a coach and sanctioned tournaments. Yufan was the real deal. The rest of us were posers.

Every time I played Yufan, I was the underdog. As you know, there is a certain kind of freedom that comes from being the underdog. I knew I wasn't going to win. He knew I wasn't going to win. Everyone watching knew I wasn't going to win. I had nothing to lose. When the game started, I was loose. I was nimble. I experimented with new serves. I tested out new ways of gripping my paddle. I felt free to try new things because the outcome of the match wasn't in question.

But every now and then, the testing, experimentation, and novel approaches would pay off. Suddenly, I'd find myself with a tie score. Or, once in a blue moon, I might even take a one-point lead.

That's when the crafty veteran would deploy some psychological warfare. Yufan would pause the game for a second. He'd open his eyes wide, cock his head back slightly, and look at me from across the table. Then, through this crooked little grin, he'd say, "Wow. You're gettin' pretty good, dude."

Suddenly, the inspiring underdog story in my mind morphed into a Greek tragedy where the would-be hero cradled victory in the palm of his hand one moment, only to watch it ooze out between the white knuckles of his clenched fist in the next. The moment I became aware that I was now the protagonist who was *expected* to win, the spunky, slingshot-wielding David became the Goliath lumbering toward my inevitable demise. I became tight and rigid and stiff. I started playing *not* to lose.

Somewhere deep in our brains we are programmed to feel very different about taking risks and trying new things once we feel like we are ahead instead of behind. In a paradoxical twist, our recent success becomes the anchor weighing down our future wins.

THE GROWTH CURVE

When we start our career, we all start at the bottom. We've got nothing to lose. We're hungry. We're willing to take risks. We're willing to experiment. We're not afraid to fall, because we just don't have that far to tumble. Not yet.

Over time, all those skinned knees teach us lessons that help us grow.

Little by little, we grow our income. We grow our social status. We grow the number of people we have the privilege of leading. For a while our confidence climbs in lockstep with our skills and our experience. We become more sure-footed and find a rhythm—*left . . . left . . . left, right, left . . .*

Then one day, as we turn around the next bend, a gust of change sweeps in and knocks us off balance. Maybe it's a reshuffling of company leadership, a dip in sales, or a job transfer. Maybe it's an opportunity you thought you always wanted, but now you're not quite sure if you're ready. Or maybe your division has been performing so spectacularly well recently that the parent

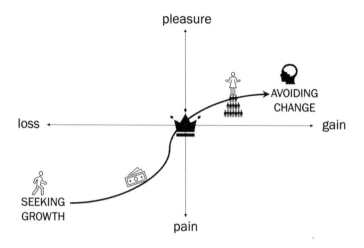

organization is suddenly asking your team to carry more of the load this year. It might even be more personal, like a change in the number of people or pets living under your roof.

Five decades of studies show that whenever we reach the top of a growth curve—in our lives, careers, finances, or companies—we're going to hear two voices.

The first voice belongs to our survival instinct. Our survival instinct tells us to pay three times more attention to what we might lose rather than what we might gain.[*] It tells us to pay three times more attention to what could go wrong rather than what could go right.

---

* The phenomenon of loss aversion was first explained in Daniel Kahneman's and Amos Tversky's "Prospect Theory: An Analysis of Decision under Risk," *Econometrica*, March 1979. I explain it in more detail in *The Impulse Factor* (Fireside, 2008). The best summary of the vast research on the topic is in Kahneman's 2013 tome *Thinking, Fast and Slow* (Farrar, Straus and Giroux).

In Javier's case, his survival instinct had started chiming in the previous year with the ouster of his firm's third partner. The third partner was a hard-charging executive who combined a knack for landing deals with a moral compass that never quite found its true north. Although the third partner's financial returns had long been impressive enough to mask his toxic personality, the reputational damage to the firm caused by his habitually amoral behavior finally proved too much for the senior partner to bear.

Although the third partner's departure was met by a collective sigh of relief inside the firm, it also raised a question about how to replace the substantial revenue he brought in.

At first, the senior partner wasn't worried. He felt confident that his remaining team had more than enough skill and brainpower to make up for the loss. But an outsized proportion of that skill and brainpower sat between Javier's temples. Suddenly, Javier was no longer just a role player. He was expected to be the rainmaker. He was expected to take the winning shot with the game on the line. Instead of filling Javier with confidence, his boss's heightened expectations surfaced his doubts. The voice of his survival instinct was screaming in his ear, day and night.

But here's the good news: One of the magical gifts of the highly evolved human brain is that when we arrive at the top of a growth curve, we don't just hear a first voice. If you listen, you'll also hear a second voice—the voice of your growth instinct. Your first voice leads with *I worry.* Your second voice begins with *I wonder.*

FIRST VOICE: I worry I don't have all the answers.
SECOND VOICE: I wonder what insights I'll discover.

FIRST VOICE: I worry I'm not qualified.
SECOND VOICE: I wonder what muscles I'll strengthen and what new skills I'll develop.

FIRST VOICE: I worry I'll disappoint the people who think so highly of me, and that I'll be exposed as a fraud.
SECOND VOICE: I wonder if all my past successes and failures, all those lessons learned, have been preparing me, like the training montage in *The Karate Kid*, to rise to an exciting challenge exactly like this one.

In the months that followed, Javier transformed his plateau into a launchpad. At the time of this writing, the senior partner has more or less turned over management of the firm to Javier, who says he's happier, healthier, wealthier, and more charitable than ever before. He's been growing. And winning. A lot.

I would love to take credit for Javier's success. But Javier would have turned this corner with or without me. This wasn't his first leap from the top of one growth curve to the start of another, and it won't be his last. All I really did for Javier was help him make that leap *sooner.* As a result he grew faster and won bigger, with less worry and more wonder. The ideas and stories in this book will help you do the same thing.

It all starts with opening your eyes to the not-so-hidden pattern behind every great thing you've ever accomplished.

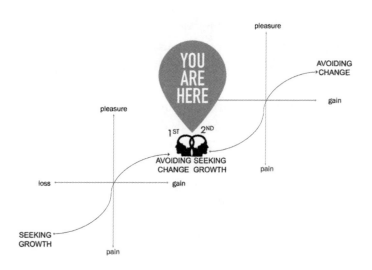

CHAPTER TWO

THE SECRET OF YOUR SUCCESS

Life must be lived forward, but it can
only be understood backward.
—Søren Kierkegaard

Think of an achievement you're really proud of. Maybe you led a team to win a sales award. Maybe you earned all-state honors in high school. Maybe you graduated near the top of your class or were selected as a first chair in the school band. Maybe you landed the lead role in a play or landed that white whale of a client in your region. Maybe you finished a marathon or secured funding from an A-list investor. Maybe you helped your child accomplish a goal they didn't believe was attainable.

How did you do it? What factors led to your triumph?

No doubt it involved some combination of talent and hard work. You probably benefited from some wise counsel from a parent, a teacher, or a mentor. Almost certainly, more than a few helping hands reached out at just the right time to pick you up and nudge you toward the next milestone.

But there was another factor you probably overlooked: change.

If we trace the timeline of your achievement, we'll likely discover it was immediately preceded by an uncomfortable season of change and uncertainty.

The year before you led your team to the conference championship, maybe you weren't even sure if you were going to make the starting lineup or recover from that future-shattering knee injury. It was precisely that change to your plans—that violation of how you expected the world to work—which altered your routine, which grew your skills, which led to that great victory.

Change happens.
You grow.
Then you win.

How about that process innovation you implemented a while back?

I'll bet you have a particular way you structure your mornings or stay connected with your customers or relate to your team members. Today, you probably take that process or habit for granted as the "obvious" right way to do things. But you haven't always done things that way. The seed of that innovation was planted during a previous season of change and uncertainty when you or someone on your team was inspired to think a little differently about the way things had always been done, which led to an insight, which grew into an innovation, which catapulted you to a new level of sustained success.

Change happens.
You grow.
Then you win.

This connection between change and achievement is no coincidence. It's a pattern. Research shows that strange and unexpected events around us act like an alarm clock that wakes up creative superpowers in our brain that most of us didn't know we had. I explained the research[*] behind this phenomenon in greater detail in my last book, *Ricochet*. For now, all you need to know is that confusion and uncertainty turn your brain into a breeding ground for insight and creativity. If necessity is the mother of invention, confusion might be the baby daddy.

My favorite example of the Change→Grow→Win pattern happened back in 1665. As a plague epidemic swept across England, an undistinguished math student returned to his childhood home after his university canceled all classes for the semester. One day while

---

* Read more about these fascinating studies in my book *Ricochet* (Beaver's Pond Press, 2017) and "The Meaning Maintenance Model: On the Coherence of Social Motivations," by Steven Heine, Travis Proulx, and Kathleen Vohs, in *Personality and Social Psychology Review*, February 2006, and "Connections from Kafka: Exposure to Meaning Threats Improves Implicit Learning of an Artificial Grammar," by Steven Heine and Travis Proulx, in *Psychological Science*, September 2009.

wandering through the apple orchard in his backyard, he noticed an apple fall from a tree. That unremarkable falling apple sparked one of the most influential ideas of modern science—the theory of gravity.

Newton had seen apples fall from trees hundreds of times before. The guy literally grew up with an apple orchard in his backyard. But it wasn't until this confusing, frustrating, and frightening period of change and uncertainty that Newton's newly unleashed creative superpowers finally connected the dots between a falling apple and the physics of gravity.

For the rest of his life, Newton looked back on that year known to history as the "Great Plague of London," and he called it his "year of wonders." Which kind of makes me wonder. What if all those questions you've been mulling over in your mind lately are not symptoms of your stress so much as they are signs that the Change→Grow→Win pattern is carrying you toward your next year of wonders?

The Change→Grow→Win pattern is like a rip current in the ocean. A rip current is a narrow channel of water that can carry unsuspecting beachgoers away from the safety of the shore and out into the sea. If you get caught in a rip current, you have three options:

Option 1. Frantically swim against the current in a desperate attempt to get back to shore. Because rip currents are nearly invisible to the untrained eye, most people don't understand why they keep drifting further from the shore even though they are swimming as hard as they can back to the dry land where they came from. So they wear themselves out, oblivious to the futility of their efforts.

Option 2. Swim to the side—parallel to the shoreline—to get out of the narrow current. Since rip currents are usually no more than twenty-five meters wide, if you spend just a minute calmly swimming to the side, you'll get out of the path of the current, where you can then paddle back to shore with little resistance. This is the standard recommendation from safety experts.

Option 3. Use the rip current like an oceanic Uber ride. That's what surfers do. Normally, surfers have to expend lots of time and energy paddling out to the spot in the ocean where the waves are breaking, while getting periodically pummeled by waves that have already broken and are now pushing them back toward the shore with tremendous speed and power. But a rip current gives surfers a Lyft to where they want to go, faster and more efficiently.

The Change→Grow→Win pattern gives you and your team those same three options.

OPTION 1: EXHAUST.

If you don't understand the pattern, you'll panic when a change starts pulling you toward the edge of your plateau at the top of your latest growth curve. You can then exhaust yourself trying to fight against the change.

OPTION 2: ESCAPE.

You can simply try to get out of the way of the pattern by side-stepping the change with early retirement, a job transfer, or quiet quitting.

OPTION 3: EMBRACE.

By better understanding the pattern, you can learn to swim with it, and let it transport you and your team to someplace rewarding and exciting at speeds that would have been impossible without it.

CHAPTER THREE

THE SPRING FEVER EFFECT

I never lose. I either win or I learn.
—Nelson Mandela

"**D**isruption is an opportunity."

That's what Michele Buck, CEO of The Hershey Company, told me multiple times on the Zoom call I had with her before I spoke to her leadership team. She wanted to make sure I really heard this core belief that has guided her successful career and helped her team double the market value of the century-old chocolate giant during her first five years at the helm.

In the past when I'd hear leaders say things like "disruption is an opportunity," my inner skeptic wondered if they were just spewing forced positivity. Was it a case of applying a fresh layer of lipstick on a pig?

But not anymore. I think sometime during her life and career, Buck learned to associate the discomfort of change with the pleasure of winning. Just like Pavlov's dogs were conditioned to salivate at the sound of a tuning fork he repeatedly paired with the delivery of savory chunks of raw meat,[*] for leaders like Buck, change and disruption have become the tuning forks signaling the delivery of a future win.

Recently, neuroscientists have found that an *anticipated* win can trigger a hit of dopamine in our brains that is even stronger than an *actual* win.[†] When disruption happens, Buck isn't just convincing herself to think happy thoughts. Disruption makes her neurons salivate, so to speak, prompting real, dopamine-induced excitement.

I call this the spring fever effect.

Every spring in the northern United States, where I grew up, the beautiful blanket of white that drapes our winter wonderland for months melts to a dirty, grayish-brown slush, revealing Big Mac wrappers, slushie straws, and orphaned mittens that some poor kindergartner dropped in the snow back in January while trudging home from school.

Despite the disappointing aesthetics, a cheery and chipper vibe known as "spring fever" spreads across the land. Why? Because sons and daughters of the tundra know the pattern. We see it unfold predictably year after year after year. The ugliness of the Big Thaw is only temporary. Before long, the garbage will get cleaned up,

---

* I. P. Pavlov, *Conditioned Reflexes* (London: Oxford University Press, 1927).

† See Wolfram Schultz's research in "Dopamine Reward Prediction Error Coding," *Dialogues in Clinical Neuroscience* 18, no. 1 (March 2016).

vibrant greens will sprout, blooming flowers will cover the landscape—and, eventually, apples will start falling from trees.

Earlier in Buck's career, after she'd proven herself a gifted marketer and a rising star in brand management at Frito-Lay, she was offered the general manager role of an entire business unit.* Technically, this was a promotion. Unfortunately, the business unit was on life support. Its unionized manufacturing plant was underperforming so profoundly that the entire division was just months away from being shuttered. On top of that, manufacturing was an area of business that Buck knew little about.

Essentially, her bosses were saying, "This is pretty much a lost cause, Michele. But if you want to take a crack at it, it's all yours."

Buck had a choice. She could stay tucked safely away in her comfort zone of branding and marketing with her proven track record of success. Or she could allow herself to be disrupted. She could step into an unfamiliar role at the bottom of an incredibly steep learning curve, surrounded by a team of people who saw her more as an adversary than an ally.

Buck's story reminded me of the offer Microsoft CEO Satya Nadella was presented with earlier in his career. His boss at the time, Steve Ballmer, asked Nadella if he wanted to try resurrecting Bing, Microsoft's flailing search engine. Along with the offer, Ballmer shared

---

* To read more about Buck's journey, read her interview in *Harvard Business Review*, "Hershey CEO Michele Buck on Empowering Internal Change Agents," April 2022.

a hard truth with his protégé: "Look, if you go to Bing and you don't do a good job or succeed, it might be your last job."[*]

The question that both Buck and Nadella had to answer was this: should I stay, or should I grow? It's the same question you must answer every time you feel the pull of the pattern.

Should I stay, or should I grow?

For leaders like Buck and Nadella, the answer comes more easily because they understand the Change→Grow→Win pattern. They have conditioned themselves to see potential disruptions like the arrival of spring. Sure, it's not pretty right now, and storms are certain ahead. But the potential for rapid growth and big wins is too great for them to pass up. The two voices inside their heads are singing a twist on the Clash's classic earworm:

> *Should I stay, or should I grow now?*
> *If I grow, there will be trouble.*
> *And if I stay, it will be double.*

If I grow, there will be trouble. Hiccups and mistakes and failures and disappointments and temporary frustrations are inevitable.

If I choose not to grow, it will be double. Inertia will usher in a frustrating decline into mediocrity, followed

---

[*] Cited in the case study by Herminia Ibarra, Aneeta Rattan, and Anna Johnston, "Satya Nadella at Microsoft: Instilling a Growth Mindset," *London Business School*, June 2018.

by a lifetime of nagging regret as you agonize over how much impact you could have made *if only* you'd had the courage and confidence to keep growing.

After leaders discover the Change→Grow→Win pattern, they perceive the world differently. In their mind's eye, the story of their life starts to look like one long series of growth curves angling up and to the right. They don't just see their present different, they also see their past and their future different.

When the call to change arrives, they see the same challenges, struggles, inconveniences, and messiness as everyone else. The difference is that they also get that hit of dopamine from anticipating all the growing and winning on the horizon. The link between *change now* and *wins ahead* is as real in their minds as the link between the smell of cool, fresh rain and the sprouting of green leaves, budding flowers, and the eventual arrival of falling apples.

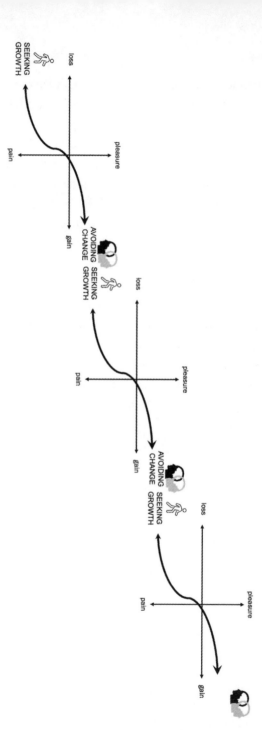

CHAPTER FOUR

THE POWER
OF A NUDGE

It ain't what you don't know that gets you into trouble.
It's what you know for sure that just ain't so.
—Mark Twain

Some years ago, a manager at IBM named Ginni Rometty had begun soaring up the corporate ladder under the tutelage of a charismatic executive named Fred Amoroso. One day, Amoroso called Rometty into his office. He explained that he'd be moving to Tokyo soon to take over IBM's service business for all of Asia-Pacific. That meant someone had to replace him to run IBM's insurance-consulting business, which Rometty had been helping him build and grow over the past four years. Amoroso told her, "I believe you should be my successor."

According to Rometty, her first thought was *Wow, that sounds wonderful. But I'm not ready*. She told Amoroso, "With another year or so, I'll be more prepared."

Amoroso just looked at her with an incredulous expression. His face said it all. *You must be kidding right now. Isn't this the promotion you've been waiting for?*

In her fascinating memoir, *Good Power*, Rometty explains, "I could have been celebrating! Instead, I was obsessing over an inner voice that said, *if only I had more knowledge, or a little more time then I can do this.* The voice then listed ten reasons why I couldn't do it versus ten reasons why I could.

"Luckily," she said, "I also heard two other voices."

She heard the voice of Fred Amoroso, who insisted that even though she didn't yet know everything she needed to know to succeed in this new role, she already knew more than enough to get started. She already possessed more than enough learning capacity to *acquire* the knowledge she'd need.

She said she also heard the voice of her husband, Mark. He reminded her of all the previous times she'd accepted a challenging new role, stretched toward a scary new goal, or agreed to embrace some other change. He reminded her of all the times in her past when she had lived the pattern.

Change happened.
She grew.
Then she won.

The following Monday morning, she accepted the job. She grew fast and won big—and continued to do so on her way to becoming the first female CEO in IBM's history and one of the most influential business leaders in the twenty-first century.

She credits this experience with teaching her a core

leadership principle: "Growth and comfort can never coexist." Just like that, Ginni Rometty caught a case of spring fever.

Upon first glance, Rometty's story might sound like the clichéd turning point in your run-of-the-mill Disney movie. It's that moment where the hero is overcome with self-doubt until a wise mentor says, "I believe in you," whereupon our hero summons the courage to rise up and make cat-posters everywhere rejoice.

But a fascinating new line of research suggests there might be something else going on here. In one set of studies, a team of researchers led by Paul O'Keefe[*] at Yale University found that a person's beliefs about growth and opportunity can have a profound impact on how they respond to change. We can believe that, no matter how talented or skilled we are (or aren't), we can't really change the number of good opportunities that come our way.

Or we can hold a belief that good opportunities can be *grown*—that it's possible to change both the quality and the quantity of opportunities that land on our doorsteps. Instead of seeing opportunities as fixed and finite, we can see opportunities as flexible and growable. During times of change, O'Keefe's team found that these beliefs produce more useful ideas. They also help us plan better; execute better; and—unsurprisingly—achieve better real-world results.

---

[*] See "Implicit Theories of Opportunity: When Opportunity Fails to Knock, Keep Waiting, or Start Cultivating?" by Paul O'Keefe, E. J. Horberg, Fiona Lee, and Carol Dweck in *Journal of Personality and Social Psychology*, June 2023.

O'Keefe's studies reveal three important factors about how the Change→Grow→Win pattern works.

1. Beliefs about the Change→Grow→Win pattern are fluid.
The people in these studies were randomly assigned to one set of beliefs or the other. It's not like the researchers went out and found a bunch of Michele Bucks, and then compared them to the unwashed masses. Only *after* people were assigned to one group did the researchers subtly suggest that one set of beliefs was truer than the other. Six different times, they randomly primed some people to believe that opportunities were fixed and finite, and primed others to believe they were flexible and growable. What this shows us is that *everyone* is capable of catching spring fever.

2. Beliefs about the pattern are surprisingly simple to alter.
It's shocking how easy it was for the researchers to influence people's basic beliefs. We often think that after spending a lifetime developing our beliefs about how the world works, we must then spend years or decades changing those beliefs. But research has convincingly shown that our mindsets are very open to suggestion. In O'Keefe's studies, all the researchers had to do to change a person's fundamental belief about the ability to grow (or not grow) opportunities was ask them eight simple questions, such as how much they agreed with a mundane statement like "It's possible that you can change how many good opportunities you have in life." The re-

searchers didn't make them watch a series of inspiring TED talks or put them through a three-month training course. They didn't even tell them what to believe. They just asked them to spend a minute rating how much they agreed with a few banal statements. Can it really be that simple? Yes.

You and I and every person in that study already have *both* mindsets inside our brains. We already hear the first voice *and* the second voice. The researchers just subtly and ever-so-slightly amplified one of those voices in the minds of their research participants. This is also why it only took a couple simple conversations for Ginni Rometty to overpower her doubts and change her mind. She didn't need to be completely reprogrammed. She just needed to turn the dial up a bit on her second voice.

3. Beliefs about the pattern only matter when things are changing, but then they matter more than most of us think.

There was no difference at all between the performance of the two groups of people in O'Keefe's study when the situation was stable and unchanging. As Warren Buffett famously quipped, it's only when the tide goes out that you get to see who was swimming naked. Stable times hide toxic beliefs.

So, the Spring Fever Effect doesn't matter much in the middle of summer. Your understanding of rip currents doesn't matter much when everyone is chilling on the beach. In stable times skill and talent can be all you need.

But when things change, our beliefs can either boost us or bury us.

The lesson for leaders, coaches, and parents is pretty simple. When change happens, instead of mindlessly repeating tired clichés like "change is hard," why not remind our teams, our partners, and ourselves that success is just as likely as failure? Why not remind them that we have more influence over our circumstances than we probably think? Why not nudge them to remember all the times before in our lives and work when the pattern has allowed us to create opportunities? Why not remind them that . . .

Change happens.
You grow.
Then you win.

CHAPTER FIVE

WHEN LIFE GIVES YOU APPLES, MAKE APPLE PIE

*Let your hook always be cast; in the pool
where you least expect it, there will be fish.*

—Ovid

One Saturday morning back in the 1960s, a few Japanese businessmen hopped on their small motorbikes and headed out to the hills west of Los Angeles to blow off some steam. Kihachiro Kawashima and his small team had arrived in the United States a couple years before to establish an American division of Honda Motor Co., Ltd.

The new venture wasn't going well.

The founders of American Honda thought they'd set a very conservative goal—snagging just a tiny slice of the American motorcycle market from Harley-

Davidson and the few European manufacturers who dominated the continent. But American bikers just didn't take to the Japanese offering. The few early adopters who deemed Honda's bikes cheap enough to try were punished with oil leaks and clutch failures. The big Honda machines that worked fine for short rides on the relatively small islands of Japan weren't ready for the endless network of open highways crisscrossing the purple mountains majesty and amber waves of grain, from sea to shining sea.

Almost two years after they arrived, with most of their big bikes already shipped back to Japan for repairs and their cash reserves running dangerously low, Kawashima's small team decided to take a break and make use of the small Honda motorbikes known as Super Cubs they'd been using to run errands around Los Angeles. Although popular with delivery drivers back on the narrow, crowded streets of urban Japan, the Honda team expected the Super Cubs to be unpopular with the Hells Angels types who characterized America's biker culture. Their suspicion was right. It was tough to put out that *Rebel Without a Cause* vibe on these scrawny machines that were half the size of a gas-guzzling Harley and sounded more like a Vespa than a Hog.

But then something unexpected happened. While tearing around the dirt roads up in the hills, the Honda team crossed paths with the ordinary, everyday Americans who were up there to hike, camp, and ride bicycles. These weren't Easy Riders in leather jackets terrorizing biker bars and frequenting established motorcycle dealers. These folks were curious about where they could score one of those interesting new "dirt bikes." At first, Kawashima and his team explained that the Super Cubs weren't available in the United States. But the curious Americans persisted, so the enterprising Japanese relented.

The rest of the story is literally a case study in business success. A couple of years later, the once-floundering American Honda was crushing the competition. They went from selling a few thousand motorcycles per year in the early 1960s to selling nearly a quarter of a million per year in 1965, and almost double that by 1970.

But here's the interesting thing: After that falling-apple moment up in the California hills, do you know what Kawashima and his team did when they arrived back in the office on Monday morning? The same thing they did the Friday before.

The insight that changed everything, changed nothing. At least not right away.

In the months that followed, American Honda kept trying—and failing—to slice off a tiny chunk of the big-bike market from Harley-Davidson. Meanwhile, one special order at a time, sales of the Super Cub kept climbing. For months and months, one-off orders of the Super Cub did nothing more than subsidize American Honda's fruitless efforts to break into the big-bike market. Finally, Kawashima and his team could no longer ignore the numbers that were practically slapping them across the face. Only then, after months and months had passed, did they put the big-bike strategy on hold and redirect their efforts toward actively selling the Super Cub.*

The story of American Honda is another great example of how change and confusion sparked game-changing insights. But it also illustrates something else about how falling apples work.

Apples need time to grow.

It took Newton twenty years to find the clarity and courage to publish his theory of gravity, an idea sparked by his first falling-apple moment. It took the Honda team months to translate their insight into an innovation.

When you retrace the steps of all your greatest achievements, you will find a trail of fallen apples that were knocked loose from their branches by some gust of change or another. The sight of each falling apple sparked a brief rush of excitement that lasted for a few hours or days. But slowly, the excitement wore off and the seed of that insight buried itself in the soil of your brain's normal daily operations. There, below the surface of your conscious thoughts, the seed germinated for weeks or months. Then one day, like a bolt from the blue, that insight sprouted up as a sapling that you nurtured and fertilized until it grew into a bona fide innovation. Over time, that innovation grew branches of its own, which

---

* To learn more about the American Honda story, check out the 2016 Harvard Business School Working Paper by Ramon Casadesus-Masanell and John Heilbron, "Decision-Making by Precedent and the Founding of American Honda." There is also a great recap in Clayton Christensen's must-read book *How Will You Measure Your Life?* (Harper Business, 2012).

produced their own apples, which eventually fell to the ground years later thanks to another gust of change. And so on.

And guess what? As you read this book, there's a high likelihood the process is underway once again. The seeds of your next great achievement are already germinating in your brain, whether or not you're aware of it. A year from now, you'll realize you're surprisingly good at doing something that, right now, you believe you can't do at all, or can't do well. Right now, the *change* around you has unleashed *growth* inside you and *wins* ahead of you.

CHAPTER SIX

FOUR LAWS AND FIVE Ws OF AGILE OPTIMISM

*To myself I am only a child playing
on the beach, while vast oceans of
truth lie undiscovered before me.*

—Isaac Newton

Our fourteen-year-old son, Franklin, had a growth spurt this past year. He went from one of the shorter kids on his volleyball team to being one of the taller kids. The additional inches prompted his coach to move him from setter (who flips the ball up in the air) to attacker (who smacks the ball back down). His role was turned upside down.

Franklin wasn't excited about the change. He'd worked hard mastering the role of setter, and he was getting a taste of success there. He was acquiring confidence and optimism, essential attributes for top performers in any endeavor. And moving to attacker felt like starting all over. To thrive in this new role, he needed a new kind of optimism.

I've discovered there are two types of optimism. *Fragile optimism* is the belief that you'll achieve a specific, desired outcome. *Agile optimism* is the belief that you'll attain a series of unexpected insights that will add up to some desirable outcome.

If Franklin's optimism at the start of the season was based solely on the expectation that every time he stepped on the court, he would meet the standard definition of success for an attacker—hit the ball squarely with enough force and accuracy to score a point—his optimism would soon be shattered. Hence the label *fragile optimism*.

Instead, Franklin's optimism needed to be based on the expectation that every time he stepped on the court, he would score *insights* that would eventually add up to winning outcomes. Maybe today he'd have an insight about the way he snapped his wrist, or the swing of his arm, or his run-up to a jump. Maybe tomorrow he'd discover something useful about reading the position of the opponent's blockers or communicating with the setter. Dozens, even hundreds, of insights are possible on any given day. But there was no way to predict ahead of time what insights would arrive or when, let alone *how* to put his discoveries into action.

In other words, Franklin had to be agile with his optimism.

Agile optimism follows four basic laws.

(Side note: My long-suffering wife claims I have

an annoying habit of "one-upping" people. Although I firmly disagree with her biased judgment, that might help to explain why Newton's theory of gravity contains three Laws of Motion and my theory of Agile Optimism contains *four* Laws of Falling Apples. Nick one, Newton zero. But who's counting?)

FIRST LAW OF AGILE OPTIMISM:
FALLING APPLES ARE SEASONAL.

We spot more falling apples during seasons of change than seasons of stability. Love it or hate it, change produces the right conditions of confusion and uncertainty for activating the powerful apple-spotting processes in our brains.

SECOND LAW OF AGILE OPTIMISM:
APPLES NEED TIME TO GROW.

The American Honda team needed months before their Super Cub insight could yield a game-changing strategy, and Newton took two decades to turn his falling apple into a groundbreaking theory. Insights aren't yet innovations, just as seeds aren't yet trees. Agile optimists endure and thrive because they savor the excitement of the falling-apple moments—even while fully aware that seeds must be buried before they can grow and be harvested months later.

THIRD LAW OF AGILE OPTIMISM:
APPLES DON'T FALL FAR FROM THE TREE.

The juiciest apples often fall just a step or two outside

the protective shade of our tree, but not so far they might have fallen from someone else's tree. It's no coincidence Newton's falling apples led him to the study of physics and calculus. The motorcycle-peddlers at American Honda had an insight about a different-sized motorbike, not about a toaster or pogo stick. Falling apples aren't magic pills that suddenly give us intelligence we didn't already possess, like Bradley Cooper in the movie *Limitless*. When you see a falling apple, it's because that juicy piece of fruit was hanging above your head in the same tree you've been standing next to all along. The difference is that a little gust of change blew in and shook the apple loose from its branch.

FOURTH LAW OF AGILE OPTIMISM: FALLING APPLES ARE PREDICTABLY UNPREDICTABLE.
Even the world's best apple growers can't predict exactly when and where the next apple will fall. And they don't need to. Trying to predict the time and location of a falling apple is an exercise in fruit-ility. But that's the point: falling apples teach us things we didn't know we needed to know. The not-knowing is what makes spotting falling apples so thrilling. It's where the wonder comes from.

Adopting an attitude of agile optimism—expecting to receive unexpected insights *before* we see the outcomes—is how we build the neural pathways that create the spring-fever effect. Relishing the mystery and anticipation is also how we can learn to *enjoy* the

Change→Grow→Win pattern, rather than just *enduring* it through groans and gritted teeth.

If we put the Change→Grow→Win pattern under the microscope, we'll see a series of Ws. But not all of these Ws are wins.

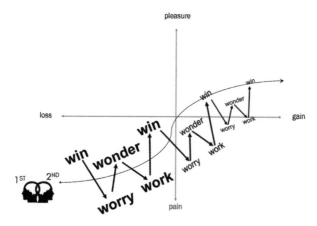

1. WIN

Growth usually starts with a win—such as a promotion, a graduation, a championship, or a sale. That win fuels our psychological engine. Franklin scored his first win when his coach demonstrated enough belief in his potential to move him directly into a scoring position. Kihachiro Kawashima scored a win when he was deemed enterprising enough to launch Honda's American division just like Ginni Rometty won when she was hand-picked as her mentor's successor.

2. WORRY

That win is quickly followed by worry. We suddenly feel the pressure of heightened expectations, or of delivering on the promise we just sold to a customer, or of continuing the winning streak, or duplicating the record-breaking performance. That pressure doesn't feel good, which is why on the growth curve it points down toward pain.

3. WONDER

Eventually our second voice speaks up, and our worry gives way to wonder. Wonder feels good, which is why it shoots us back up toward pleasure on the growth curve. But it's not yet a real-world win so it doesn't quite rise to the same height as the win that came before it.

4. WORK

Wonder gives us a clue about where to point our efforts next, which reenergizes us for more work. Although work isn't always pleasurable, work is what turns a wonder into a win. Which is why the work arrow points toward pain and gain on the growth curve.

5. WIN

After doing the work of putting our latest insight into action, we score another win. And as we all know, winning feels great.

The five Ws help explain why it can be hard to see the Change→Grow→Win pattern working when we're in the middle of it. We believe worry signals a problem.

Every few weeks, Franklin would experience a mini-breakthrough in his hitting. Something new would click and his performance in a practice or a game would surge ahead. Naturally, he would come home feeling excited—like he'd finally turned a corner in his development.

But then, just like clockwork, a few practices or games later he would come home disappointed. He felt like he was backsliding. And technically, his performance had dropped a bit from his newly established peak. But it was still higher than his previous peak from the month before. That's how the growth process works. By recognizing that he was simply in another temporary Worry phase of the 5 Ws, Franklin could calm his nerves. He could breathe easier knowing that another Wonder was on its way, and an even higher peak was on the horizon.

Researchers at the University of Chicago* have found that people overwhelmingly believe changes for better are just temporary flukes, but slight changes for worse are signs of an irreversible downward spiral. When one project falls a few days behind, we immediately conclude that this is the dead canary in the coal mine of our

---

* In "Do 70 Per Cent of All Organizational Change Initiatives Really Fail?" (*Journal of Change Management* 11, 2011), University of Brighton researcher Mark Hughes thoroughly debunked this zombie statistic that refuses to die. After I wrote a widely read article about the dubious origins of this statistic for Harvard Business Review in 2018—"Stop Using the Excuse 'Organizational Change is Hard'"—and was then asked to record a video on the same topic for the Harvard Mentor Management training program, I thought my crusade had suceeded. But five years later during the writing of this book, the stat rose from the dead again in a cover story in . . . wait for it . . . *Harvard Business Review*. [*Insert the hand-slapping-forehead emoji here*]. The fact this phony failure rate won't stay dead shows just how strong our bias against positve change truly is.

doomed change project . . . never mind all the wins we've earned in the weeks and months before.

A few years ago, it was this University of Chicago study that sent me on a one-man crusade to get leaders, pundits, and consultants to stop citing phony statistics that say "70 percent of organizational change initiatives end in failure" and "80 percent of New Year's resolutions fail by February." Never mind that these statistics have no more basis in fact than unicorns and leprechauns. Never mind we now have plenty of evidence to suggest they create a harmful self-fulfilling prophecy in our teams and our organizations. Our first-voice beliefs are drawn to these numbers like hungry mosquitoes are drawn to hikers at sunset.

The good news is that the University of Chicago researchers found the same thing Paul O'Keefe's team found. When the Chicago researchers gave people a simple reminder that change for the better is, in fact, just as likely as change for the worse, their negative bias completely vanished.

When we start making agile optimism our default setting like Michele Buck or Satya Nadella has, we don't start expecting an uninterrupted string of victories on the road ahead. We just start expecting to find a trail of falling apples that will gradually lead us toward another big win. Every worry, every lesson, every rejection, every insight, every failure, every false start is just one more falling apple helping us grow faster on our way to winning bigger.

CHAPTER SEVEN

THROW KOKOMO A STICK

Time is the longest distance between two places.
—Tennessee Williams

When I was growing up, we had this adorable little dog. We named her Kokomo because this brown, black, and white bundle of joy entered our family right around the time the Beach Boys released their chart-topping hit of the same name.

Kokomo was a cross between a wiener dog and a basset hound whose fully perked ears wouldn't even reach your kneecaps. But anytime someone came within 100 meters of our front doorstep, Kokomo bounced and barked and growled like she was White Fang about to engage in a fight to the death with an Alaskan grizzly bear.

If someone happened to knock on the door when I was lying on the living room floor with my head propped up on an elbow, trying to catch the exciting conclusion to that week's episode of *Growing Pains* or *Miami Vice*, Kokomo's barking was incredibly annoying. After all, we lived in the middle of nowhere, surrounded by rows of corn as far as the eye could see, in an area with a crime rate of approximately 0.0000001 percent. Kokomo was overreacting, to say the least.

On the other hand, it was also kind of sweet and heartwarming to know that this cute, feisty little mutt wanted nothing more in the world than to protect my two brothers, my sister, and me. I took quiet comfort in knowing that Kokomo was our ever-present early warning system.

Your survival instinct is like Kokomo. It is a loyal lookout trying to protect you—not a demon to be exorcised. It just overreacts sometimes.

The good news is we can positively redirect our survival instinct's nervous energy the same way we did with Kokomo.

Basset hounds were bred for hunting hares in France hundreds of years ago. So Kokomo was literally born and bred to pick up a scent and then chase it down. If we were out in the backyard and I wanted to direct her attention away from the alarming odor of an unexpected visitor, all I had to do was hurl an object through the air. A ball, a stick, a Frisbee, a newspaper. It didn't matter. I just had to give her something to chase.

The same is true for your survival instinct.

To help Javier get off his plateau, we had to give his brain something to chase. I asked him to write a description of his future self, ten years down the road, using prompts such as:

Javier is . . .
Javier has accomplished . . .
Javier spends his days doing . . .
Javier's relationship with his wife looks like . . .
Javier's relationship with his eighteen-year-old daughter
    looks like . . .
Javier's relationship with his fifteen-year-old son looks
    like . . .

Social scientists call this technique "self-distancing." It turns out that one of the simplest ways to overcome our momentary fears and frustrations is to take a long-term view of our short-term situation—to project ourselves into a distant time and place.

I created Javier's prompts based on my previous conversations and assessments about what was most important to him. But anything that helps you write about yourself from a distanced perspective can do the trick.

Write your own obituary. Ask your team to write a press release about the imagined future completion of an important project or goal. These can trigger that same distancing effect. Effective self-distancing prompts rely on two main ideas:

1. LOOKING AT THE CURRENT SITUATION FROM A FUTURE PERSPECTIVE.

I find it works best to describe some vivid details of that future place. For example, I asked Javier to write about the relationship his future self would have with his eighteen-year-old daughter and fifteen-year-old son, because his kids were only eight and five at the time. I wanted him to really imagine the passage of time and what ten years down the road would actually look and feel like for him.

2. WRITE ABOUT THE SITUATION USING THE THIRD-PERSON POINT OF VIEW.

Yes, it feels a little silly to write something like "Nick has become a role model for brave risk-taking" instead of "I am a role model for brave risk-taking." But studies suggest that my brain really does treat "Nick" as a different person than "I."

When a young Jeff Bezos was deciding whether to give up his promising career trajectory as an investment banker to start Amazon, he says he imagined which option his eighty-year-old self would regret more—giving this idea a try or letting it pass him by. That was a specific kind of distancing using time as the variable. Later, Bezos famously implemented a variation of the distancing technique when he required that one chair at every Amazon meeting must be left open to represent the voice of the customer. While "the customer" never actually spoke, thinking about the perspective of the imagined person sitting in the empty chair created a little dose of self-distancing for the people who were present. They were constantly reminded to imagine how other people—end users—might weigh in on their situation. When their first voice said something like "It would be a lot easier if we just design our shopping cart to work like our competitors' carts," that imaginary customer might have amplified their second voice: "Yes, it'll take more work. But how cool would it be if we could whittle down the checkout process to a single click?"

When the prospect of change knocks, and your survival instinct immediately barks to scare off the intruder, your growth instinct throws a stick for your survival instinct to chase.

CHAPTER EIGHT

WHAT WOULD UNCLE HANK DO?

My motto was always to keep swinging. Whether I was in a slump or feeling badly or having trouble off the field, the only thing to do was keep swinging.
—Hank Aaron

When Wonya Lucas took over as the CEO of Crown Media in 2021, she was tasked with changing the public perception of her new employer. Specifically, they needed to include more underrepresented populations in their flagship brand—Hallmark Channel's snowy-white Christmas movies. While many applauded the move, Lucas also faced heavy criticism and even threats of physical violence.

To keep herself confident and focused, Lucas says she often thought about the year of wonders experienced by her famous uncle, Hank Aaron. During Aaron's record-breaking season back in the 1970s, he received a barrage of death threats for having the audacity to be a Black man trying to break the great Babe Ruth's home run record. Aaron's children—Lucas's older cousins—even had to be sent home from college for a semester because of the death threats they were receiving in their dorm rooms. Throughout it all, Lucas remembered how Uncle Hank remained calm and confident by focusing on his future goal of breaking barriers and making history. His example gave her a psychological blueprint for navigating her own barrier-breaking endeavors.

We all have our own version of an Uncle Hank.

My Uncle Hank was my mom. I was a late bloomer who struggled in sports in my early years of high school. (More on that later on in the epilogue). My mom was also a late bloomer who loved sports. Even though her basketball coaches didn't think the barely five-foot-tall ninth grader had any real potential, she shot hundreds of free throws every day, month after month, year after year. By the time she finally hit a little bit of a growth spurt, she'd turned herself into such an undeniably good shooter that the coaches simply couldn't ignore her. By junior year, she was the team's leading scorer. As team captain her senior year, she led her team to the state tournament.

As I experienced crushing defeat after crushing defeat during those first two years of high school, it was largely my mom's example that kept me going.

I bet you have an Uncle Hank too. Maybe a grandparent who not only survived the Great Depression but built a thriving career in its aftermath? Maybe a coach or career mentor whose unique sense of humor or uncommon empathy helped your team rise to an unexpected level of performance?

Here's the most powerful spin on the Uncle Hank story: *You* will be somebody else's Uncle Hank one day. The decisions you're making *right now* about how to talk, think, and behave at the top of your current growth curve will someday provide the road map for one of your kids or your peers or your team members.

CHAPTER NINE

THE TROUBLE WITH RESILIENCE

We are like eggs. You cannot go on indefinitely being just an ordinary, decent egg. We must be hatched or go bad.

—C.S. Lewis

I want to take a brief intermission here to clarify the role resilience plays in the Change→Grow→Win pattern. We often think of unflappable employees, leaders, and teams as the antidote to wobbly markets, unstable regulatory environments, technology disruptions, and global chaos. In the stories you've read so far, resilience certainly played a role.

But resilience has a downside.

A recent study found that some people are genetically predisposed to bounce back from everything from unstable home environments to outright child abuse.* A valuable trait, no doubt.

---

* See "Genetic Moderation of Intervention Efficacy: Dopaminergic Genes, the Incredible Years, and Externalizing Behavior in Children," *Child Development* 88, no. 3 (May 2017).

But the researchers also found something else. Many of those same Steady Eddies who were immune to adversity also failed to benefit from potentially positive changes. It seems that no matter what happened to these resilient kids—good, bad, or ugly—they remained unchanged.

The problem with this kind of resilience is that sometimes bouncing back to our original form isn't the optimal response to change. It can be great for survival, but it can be a huge roadblock for the Change→Grow→Win pattern. So, in that way, resilience can be the enemy of personal growth and organizational transformation.

In practice, there are two kinds of resilience: chameleon resilience and caterpillar resilience.

Chameleon resilience is what you probably think about when you hear the term *resilience*: the power of a body to return to its original form or position after being bent, compressed, or stressed. This kind of resilience wants you to batten down the hatches, shore up your defenses, and make just enough skin-deep changes to blend in or slide by until the change passes.

Chameleon resilience is always the preferred choice of your survival instinct. When I first started coaching him, Javier was trying to be a chameleon. He was logging eighty-hour weeks on projects that were easily controlled, presented almost no risk of failure, and required no substantial changes to the role he played in the firm. Never mind the minimal impact those projects would have on the growth and success of his firm or the slow-motion train wreck the chameleon approach was having on his career, his relationships, and the legacy he wanted to create. To his great credit, he recognized that something more was needed.

Caterpillar resilience is the other kind of resilience. This form of adapting to change is about letting yourself get swallowed by a cocoon before popping out a while later as something new and different. Caterpillar resilience is what happens when you choose to listen to the voice of your growth instinct.

To be clear, chameleon resilience is far better than no resilience at all. For those kids in the resilience study, surviving abuse and chronic instability with their sanity still intact was an enormous victory.

However, sometimes the change happening around us is an invitation to grow something inside us.

These changes invite us to do more than put new curtains on the window. They urge us to take a sledge-hammer to the wall between the kitchen and the family room, pull up the flooring, yank out the toilet, and create an entirely new living space.

CHAPTER TEN

THE PSYCHOLOGY OF AGILE LEADERSHIP

A different language is a different vision of life.
—Federico Fellini

Now that you have a deeper understanding of how the change-grow-win pattern works, I hope you're starting to see change management a little differently. Change is a reality every leader must manage, but *also* a golden opportunity every leader should leverage. It is an opportunity to lead the people around you through a year of wonders.

Leading a year of wonders starts with understanding the difference between change management and agile leadership. Change management is persuading your people to do what the organization wants them to do. Agile leadership is helping your people want to do what they need to do to grow faster and win bigger.

Change management is about enduring change. Agile leadership is about embracing change.

Let's unpack that.

*Agile leadership **helps your people** want to do what they need to do to grow faster and win bigger.*

It's not about forcing your people to sacrifice themselves for the organization or merely fall in line with top-down directives. It's about showing them how this way forward can advance their career, realize their potential, or help them achieve something else they desire (e.g., money, autonomy, flexibility).

*Agile leadership helps your people **want to do** what they need to do to grow faster and win bigger.*

Old-school change management has gotten pretty good

at creating systems that get people to do what they're told. But that model creates compliant doers, not creative thinkers. Team members who *want to* spot opportunities—and who get energized by finding new ways forward—enhance your team's speed and agility more than those who sit back and wait for the leader to spot each apple, cut it up, and hand them their slice.

*Agile leadership helps your people want to do **what they need to do** to grow faster and win bigger.*

On the diagram, the change management circle sits inside the agile leadership circle. That's because agile leadership *includes* change management. To be agile, your team members will often need to do what the organization needs them to do even if it's not what they want in that moment—and even if it's not immediately obvious how each specific task will directly help that person grow or win. Folding the laundry and doing the dishes aren't directly helping my kids grow faster and win bigger in the areas they currently care about—school, sports, friends, etc. But these tasks are essential for our family system to function. And our family system is the primary support for growth and development they *do* care about. Same is true in an organization.

*Agile leadership helps your people want to do what they need to do **to grow faster and win bigger**.*

The goal of agile leadership is to help your team grow faster and win bigger. The goal is not comfort. As you already know, growing and winning can be fun, exciting, and personally fulfilling. But as Ginni Rometty discovered, "growth and comfort can never coexist." That's why agile leaders are good coaches but not great cruise ship captains. Agile leaders condition their teams to embrace the tension, confusion, and discomfort that cruise ship captains go to great lengths to help their passengers avoid.

The remaining chapters will help you lead with more agility by showing you how to help your team embrace change—to want to do what they need to do to be successful in this changing environment. You need to give them three things:

1. Continuity
2. Clarity
3. Confidence

CHAPTER ELEVEN

CONTINUITY:

LINKING THE FUTURE DREAM WITH THE FOUNDING IDENTITY

*A people without the knowledge of
their past history, origin and culture
is like a tree without roots.*

—Marcus Garvey

One gray winter day a while back, my wife and I had a falling-apple moment on the drive home from our visit to a marriage counselor.

It wasn't that Alison and I were fighting a lot, or because any specific grievance had wedged itself between us. Both of us were simply in a hard-to-define *funk*. Maybe it was the recent discovery that we were having a fourth baby when we had thought we were almost done with diapers. Or maybe it was just the lack of sunlight in Minnesota in February. Who knows.

We couldn't put our finger on exactly what it was, and we were both trying hard not to point our fingers at each other. Whatever the source of our malaise, both of us were hearing nothing but the echoes of our first voice telling us something wasn't quite right.

But on the drive home that day, we started to hear our second voices. Our second voices told us that the one common thread woven through all the best times in our relationship—the times we felt closest—weren't when we had the most money or the most free time. Our relationship was always the strongest when we were both working hard to realize a *shared* future dream.

By temperament, Alison and I are both driven and competitive. If left unchecked, each of us can become so driven toward our own independent goals that we unintentionally start competing with each other for time, affection, resources, and mindshare. For us, having a shared future dream is not just an inspiring way to make our lives more interesting (although that's true too); it's a necessity for keeping us both on the same track. Every high-performing team I've ever worked with lives in that same context.

What occurred to us on that dreary drive home is that Alison and I had no shared future dream at that moment. The last one happened in the wake of the 2008 financial crisis a few years earlier. That change inspired a decision to become debt-free by the time we turned thirty-five years old. For about three years, "DebtFree35" was our mantra—and our password for everything from our Netflix log-ins to our bank accounts.

Eventually, we made it. We realized our debt-free dream. Yay for us!

The problem is we didn't replace that dream with a new aspiration. We just sat there perched atop our debt-free growth curve, pinching pennies and praying we didn't backslide.

We needed to throw a stick for ourselves. We needed a new dream to chase and a new growth curve to start climbing. But what would it be?

Eventually, we dusted off an old dream to live somewhere outside of the continental United States for an extended period. One of the common interests that brought us together in the first place was a love for travel. We first met after we'd each independently uprooted our lives from the upper Midwest to move to Southern California for no reason other than wanting to. Then, instead of spending our honeymoon at an all-inclusive resort or taking a romantic cruise, we backpacked around Europe, spending our nights in youth hostels and our days missing trains, getting lost on the streets of ancient cities, and feeding ourselves to a hungry pack of bedbugs in an elderly Dutch woman's spare bedroom in Amsterdam. And we loved every minute of it. That felt like an important clue about what made us tick and where we should look for our next big goal.

Although I didn't know it at the time, new studies* show that the most compelling change visions also look to the past. Contrary to what most people think, effective visions of change and transformation do *not* emphasize

---

* See "Visions of Change as Visions of Continuity," *Academy of Management Journal*, 62, no. 3 (June 2019).

how things will be different than the past. Instead, they highlight how the new plan will restore key elements of the past. That's what CEO Angela Ahrendts did during her transformation of Burberry in the early 2000s when she shared a vision of returning the storied fashion brand to its "British heritage" and emphasizing the company's role as the inventor of trench coats. Ahrendts's leadership team brought Burberry back to relevance in the new millennium by emphasizing its founding ideas from a century before.

That's also what Alan Mulally did in 2006. The new CEO spent hours combing through the company's archives where he found a 1925 advertisement featuring Henry Ford's original vision to "open the highways to all mankind." For the tens of thousands of Ford employees whose personal identity was closely linked to the company's identity, Mulally's change vision was actually reassuring, rather than threatening. That's why story after story of successful transformation begins with change leaders building a bridge between the company's original identity and the future dream.

In our view, Alison and I were not making a break from our past so much as we were reclaiming our true identities as travelers and explorers.

A few minutes later, while looking through our snowflake-dotted windshield at a sea of fellow travelers speeding along Interstate 694 north of Minneapolis, we decided to put a goal date on the calendar. By September 1, 2016, we would embark on a family adventure somewhere outside the continental United States.

If I wasn't fully aware of how unreliable human memory can be, I'd swear the clouds suddenly parted and the sun lit up the car the moment we made that decision.

We still had no idea where we were going or how we'd manage the logistics—of the move, of our careers while we were away, all of it. But we gave ourselves eighteen months to figure out the details. We trusted that if we just kept moving forward, we'd see the right falling apples at the right time to make it all happen.

In the end, the details didn't matter as much as our renewed excitement about reclaiming our true identities and chasing the same stick.

CHAPTER TWELVE

CLARITY:

CLARIFY YOUR COFFEE BY CUTTING YOUR SANDWICHES

The problem with communication . . . is the illusion that it has been accomplished.
—George Bernard Shaw

A while back, Starbucks found themselves at the top of a growth curve.

After two decades of legendary growth, Starbucks sales had finally started sputtering. Their incredible success popularized gourmet coffee on a global scale. Their success, naturally, attracted a horde of competitors, apparently putting a ceiling on Starbucks's meteoric rise.

One day during that time, the chain's founder and former CEO Howard Schultz walked into a Starbucks location in downtown Seattle. When he let go of the wooden handle on the glass door and stepped inside, he wasn't greeted by the scent of freshly brewed coffee. He was assaulted by the odor of burnt cheddar cheese. Some cheese had melted off one breakfast sandwich, dripped onto the oven grates, and then continued burning with each sandwich served that day.[*]

Personally, I can tell you that the smell of toasted cheese makes *my* mouth water. But for Schultz—at this pivotal moment in the life cycle of the mature coffee company he'd launched two decades earlier and then nurtured for twenty years—the smell of burnt cheese in his coffee shops was as foul as the odor of rotting flesh from a gangrenous thigh.

In the months leading up to this, Schultz had already been listening to the voice of his growth instinct. He'd zoomed out and realized the chain's best bet for future growth was reconnecting with its coffee roots. He'd been telling his people, "We need to reassert our coffee authority." Just like Angela Ahrendts and Alan Mulally, Howard Schultz intuitively understood the psychological power of that promise to restore the company's "true identity."

But his message wasn't getting through.

Sure, people were nodding in agreement. But what else are you supposed to do when the head honcho at the coffee company that pays your bills tells you to focus on coffee? *After all*, you think, *we're all trying to sell more coffee every day already, aren't we?* But just because people say they agree doesn't mean they truly understand.

Walking into that store on that fateful day was a fall-

---

[*] See Schultz's 2012 memoir *Onward* (Rodale, 2011) for more.

ing apple moment for Schultz. He finally knew what he had to do.

A few months later, he took one of the company's most popular and profitable products—breakfast sandwiches—and pulled them from the shelves of all sixteen thousand Starbucks stores. Wall Street analysts thought he'd lost his mind.

But how do you think that instant burst of clarity impacted the people working at Starbucks?

It was like a shock to the system. Suddenly, employees and managers throughout Starbucks started seeing falling apples everywhere they looked—in the way they merchandised their stores; the way they poured espresso shots; the way they built connections with the customers who walked up to their counter every day looking for a pick-me-up.

During that year of wonders, Starbucks unleashed a torrent of coffee-based innovations that jumpstarted their stalling growth engine once again. Eighteen months later, Starbucks logged its best year ever. And again the next year. And the year after that. And the year after that.

So, what's *your* team's coffee? What are *your* breakfast sandwiches?

CHAPTER THIRTEEN

CONFIDENCE:

PUSH AND LOVE

*To be a leader in this company, your job is
to find the rose petals in a field of shit.*
—Satya Nadella

Back in spring 2016, Microsoft unveiled a chatbot named Tay. Within hours of taking Tay live on Twitter, trolls had figured out that if they kept overwhelming Tay's learning with sexist and racist remarks, Tay would start spitting those slurs back out. Within a day, Tay produced ninety-six thousand tweets that got more and more offensive by the minute before Tay's creators realized what was happening and took it down. The press blasted Microsoft, calling this early experiment in artificial intelligence "a humiliation" that "failed by its own standards."

How did Microsoft's recently appointed CEO, Satya Nadella, respond to this public humiliation?

He personally wrote to Tay's creators telling them to "keep pushing, and know that I am with you."[*]

At any other company, Nadella's supportive response might not have been noteworthy. But this was Microsoft, whose famous cofounder, Bill Gates, became notorious for responding to his team's suggestions and brainstorms with "that's the stupidest f***ing idea I've ever heard."

For many years, Gates's single-minded focus on finding and elevating only the smartest people and ideas had helped create one of the world's most successful companies. But over time, that high-performance culture devolved. Eventually, the smartest thing you could do as a Microsoft employee was hide your mistakes and call attention to others' missteps so you'd look smarter by comparison. Microsoft became the exact opposite of an agile, growth-minded culture.

Nadella grew up in that culture, having spent his entire career at Microsoft. But he knew it had to change. In 2014, when he was named the third CEO in its history, Microsoft had been stranded at the top of the same growth curve for nearly fifteen years. To get its 128,000 employees to finally start climbing a new growth curve, Nadella needed to make the voice of the growth instinct inside the company louder than the voice of the survival instinct.

His response to Tay's creators after that failure is one small example of how he amplified the growth instinct

---

[*] I found this quote in the same excellent London Business School case study by Herminia Ibarra, Aneeta Rattan, and Anna Johnston that I referenced earlier, "Satya Nadella at Microsoft: Instilling a Growth Mindset" (June 2018).

with what I think of as a "push-and-love" leadership style.

Before I spoke to a large gathering of Walmart's regional managers recently, I got to hear from a retiring leader named Dacona Smith. Smith's amazing career began as a teenaged cart-coraller in Dallas, where he worked alongside his mom, who was a cashier. And it culminated decades later as chief operating officer overseeing 1.2 million employees. Smith attributes much of his success as a leader to a simple principle he learned years earlier from his high school basketball coach: a good leader will "push you hard with one arm, while loving you with the other arm."

After spending most of my career as an organizational psychologist studying change and leadership, I can think of no better guiding principle—**great leaders of change push you with one arm and love you with the other arm.**

If you only push and shove, you're just being a bully.

If you only hug and love—but never push—you aren't helping your people reach their potential as human beings or professionals.

Great leaders push *and* love.

Here's why: What looks like complacency is often just the disguise people wear to hide a lack of confidence. When we don't believe we have what it takes to successfully make a change, we try to convince ourselves (and each other) that change isn't really necessary. It's like faking an injury to avoid losing a game or pretending you don't actually like that person you're smitten with so you don't risk rejection.

The push-and-love approach pushes you to do the thing you're scared to do—not out of fear, but because your leader's confidence in you convinces you that you have what it takes to succeed. Pushing and loving is exactly what Satya Nadella was doing when he wrote to Tay's creators, "keep pushing, and know that I am with you." What message do you think that sent to all of Microsoft's employees about climbing a new growth curve—about trying new things to grow faster and win bigger?

Later that year, Tay's creators launched a new troll-resistant chatbot named Zo. As of 2024, Microsoft is leading the way in AI. Nadella's push-and-love handling of that "humiliating" failure was just one example of how he unleashed Microsoft's growth potential. His approach led to their winning position in the biggest technological revolution of the twenty-first century.

By pushing people with one arm and loving them with the other, good leaders give their people the confidence needed to embrace change so they can grow faster and win bigger.

CHAPTER FOURTEEN

BROADCAST ROOSEVELT'S *BUT*

The only thing we have to fear is fear itself.
—Franklin Delano Roosevelt

One spring day in early March of 1933, the newly elected president of the United States, Franklin Delano Roosevelt, stepped up to the lectern on the east portico of the US Capitol Building and delivered his inaugural address. Of the 1,833 words FDR spoke that day, only ten became immortalized.

"The only thing we have to fear is fear itself."

But do you know what he said right before that?

"This is preeminently the time to speak the truth, the whole truth, frankly and boldly." He doesn't sugarcoat what he describes as the "dark realities of the moment."

But there is a but.

He then says, "let me assert my firm belief that the only thing we have to fear is fear itself—nameless, unreasoning, unjustified terror which paralyzes needed efforts to convert retreat into advance."

A minute later he follows the same pattern when he says:

"... a host of unemployed citizens face the grim problem of existence. . . .

"Yet our distress comes from no failure of substance. We are stricken by no plague of locusts . . . Plenty is at our doorstep."

Over and over again it is: Reality but hope. Reality but hope. Reality but hope.

FDR's "but" is a secret weapon for helping you and the people around you fully embrace change.

By the time Roosevelt took office, the Great Depression had been plaguing the people of the United States for three long and devastating years. When Americans looked out at the shuttered banks down the street and the empty cupboards inside the kitchens of their unheated houses, they saw few signs that things were getting any better. People were afraid.

If FDR completely ignored the survival instinct blasting inside people's heads, his message of hope and courage would've been dismissed as the ravings of a "foolish optimist." Worse still, given that Roosevelt famously belonged to one of the richest families in America, a message of unqualified optimism from their new fat-cat president might have been received by the hungry masses of America the same way the French proletariat received Marie Antoinette's "let them eat cake." Instead of becoming the only four-term president in US history,

FDR might have become the only president to have his head unceremoniously separated from his body.

Luckily for his nation (and his head), Roosevelt and his speechwriters followed this formula:

"_____"

First voice: Clarify the reality.

but

"_____"

Second voice: Spotlight the potential.

This speech pattern pops up over and over again in the language of effective leaders.

Thanks to our well-trained survival instinct, leaders usually have no trouble nailing the "dark realities" part of the message. But it's easy to forget about the future potential part. So, they end up creating a burning platform that makes their people want to jump ship.

On sunnier days, leaders might get the "nothing to fear but fear" part right, but they forget to acknowledge the dark realities of the present. As a result, they either end up creating a dangerously complacent team or get themselves branded as naive and out of touch.

The magic happens when we use "but" to link first-voice realities with the second-voice possibilities.

CHAPTER FIFTEEN

BURNING PLATFORMS AND LIGHTING TORCHES

The job of a leader is to define reality and give hope.
—Ken Chenault

One summer evening back in 1988, a gas pump exploded on an oil drilling rig one hundred twenty miles off the coast of Aberdeen, Scotland. Near the stroke of midnight, three roughnecks faced a horrifying decision. They could stay on deck with smoke filling their lungs, encircled by a fire so hot it was melting steel machinery. Or they could jump off the ten-story deck into the bone-chilling water of the North Sea that was now dotted with huge chunks of metal debris.

One of the men chose to stay on deck. The other two leapt from the burning platform. The jumpers survived the plunge and were picked up by a rescue boat minutes later. The man who stayed on the platform perished in the fire.

"It was either jump or fry," the survivors explained to a reporter.

Thus was born one of the most enduring metaphors in modern business: *the burning platform*.

The burning platform idea says that if leaders want people to do something new and different—to take the plunge—they need to set fire to the ground under those people's feet. Otherwise, the thinking goes, they won't be able to resist the urging of their first voice, and they'll continue white-knuckling the status quo.

But is that true? Will scaring your team into jumping deliver the results you want? The scientific research on fear as a motivator shows:

Fear is good at scaring people *out of complacency*.
Fear is bad at scaring people *into creativity*.

For example, a recent set of experiments by Kyle Emich and Lynne Vincent found that teams driven by fear and pressure—teams who were primed by the researchers to listen to their survival instinct—were quicker to act than teams who felt optimistic and excited about the future.[*]

Score one for the burning platform.

However, those same fearful teams generated *fewer*

---

[*] See "Shifting Focus: The Influence of Affective Diversity on Team Creativity" in *Organizational Behavior and Human Decision Processes* 156 (January 2020).

solutions overall, and the solutions those teams came up with were obvious and didn't change anything.

Fear exists to help us survive immediate danger. It narrows our vision and focuses our energy on a single urgent act. When a snarling bear woke up in the back of the cave that our ancestors called home, there was no time to gather Urg and Glug for an impromptu whiteboard session. Fear told our fittest-for-survival ancestors to *drop the cave paint and get those Flintstone feet spinning.* Even today, fear can motivate. If all you want is for Dave in accounting to break his addiction to the old filing system and *download the new app already, Dave!*, then a "jump or fry" ultimatum might do the trick.

But when creativity is the goal, fear often fails to generate the innovative solutions that help us grow faster and win bigger. Here's a good rule of thumb:

The survival instinct responds to *jump-or-fry* ultimatums.

The growth instinct responds to *dream-and-fly* suggestions.

Instead of only explaining how catastrophic it will be to lose the space race, why not also illustrate how exciting it will be to put a person on the moon?

Instead of only scaring our people about the dangers of not taking a plunge, why not also make them feel safe enough to take some risks?

Instead of only burning the platform, why not also light a torch?

CHAPTER SIXTEEN

BEST DAY EVER

*The world is full of magic things patiently
waiting for our senses to grow sharper.*
—William Butler Yeats

With tears welling up in their eyes, our three boys—Rueben (ten years old), Franklin (eight years old), and Lincoln (five years old)—climbed out of our minivan like Allied soldiers landing on the beaches of Normandy. It was January 2018, and this was their first day at a new school. But this wasn't just any new school. This was a Spanish-speaking school in Puerto Rico.

Technically, the school branded itself as "bilingual." But calling this school bilingual was sort of like calling McDonald's an Asian-fusion restaurant because you can order soy sauce with your McNuggets. This was a Spanish school with a dollop of English. Our Minnesota-born sons didn't read, speak, or understand Spanish. As if the language barrier wasn't nerve-wracking enough, my kids were also only three of four total non–Puerto Ricans of any age at this K–12 school.

At this point, you're probably wondering why Alison

and I forced our kids to do this. Good question. Contrary to my sons' hypothesis, we weren't sadists who enjoyed watching our children suffer. So, let me back up.

Remember our shared future dream to live somewhere outside the continental United States for a year? The plan had been to live in Puerto Rico for twelve months. During that year, we decided to homeschool the kids for two reasons. First, we wanted to have our days as free as possible to explore the island during our little sabbatical. Second, we weren't aware of any English-speaking schools in the city where we lived, and our kids spoke no Spanish.

When that one-year adventure finished on September 1, 2017, we flew back to Minneapolis just as planned. We had heads full of memories and terabytes full of digital photos and videos.

That was supposed to be that.

Just two weeks later, Hurricane Maria swept through the Caribbean and ravaged Puerto Rico. Thousands of miles away in Minnesota, as news coverage of the wreckage filled the headlines, everyone told us, "Wow, you guys sure dodged a bullet!"

Our first voice responded, "Yeah, I guess we got out just in time."

Then our second voice said, "But I wonder . . ."

I wonder how our friends and neighbors are getting along in the wake of this disaster? I wonder what we could be doing to help if we were still there? I wonder what our kids could learn about the value of stepping outside your comfort zone to be in service of something bigger than yourself?

Over the next few weeks, that second voice grew more insistent. *I wonder what would happen if we went back . . .*

Going back wasn't part of the plan. How did we know we weren't just getting swept up by an intense case of survivor's guilt? How would we know which voice we were supposed to listen to? There was no way to know. So, we did the only thing we could. We watched and waited to see if any apples would fall.

The first apple was an invitation for me to deliver a keynote speech in Lima, Peru, for a global pharmaceutical company. Even though this had absolutely nothing to do with Puerto Rico, it seemed noteworthy since I'd never been invited to speak in Latin America.

Improbably, a few weeks later, I received a second, completely unrelated invitation to speak to a group of human resources professionals in Santiago, Chile. This was officially the second time I had been invited to speak in Latin America. Coincidence? Maybe.

Then in November—after doing zero business in Puerto Rico for the entire year we lived there—I was approached by a German pharmaceutical company to coach an engineering leader at a manufacturing plant in the exact city in Puerto Rico where we'd lived the previous year.

The rapid succession of these three notable events over the course of a three-month time frame felt an awful lot like the universe was raining apples down on our heads. The skeptic in me wondered if we were being fooled by randomness. The believer in me wondered if we were being guided by God. The psychologist in me wondered if my wife and I were just two people with a bad case of wanderlust inventing ways to rationalize our impulses. Feel free to draw your own conclusions.

Whatever the true motivations, we made a decision. In the middle of a mass exodus in which nearly one-fifth of the island's residents were leaving to escape rolling blackouts, an unpredictable water supply, and near-constant shortages of gas, groceries, and everything else, Alison and I decided to move our family of six back to Puerto Rico.

Only this time, the primary goal of our move wasn't exploration: it was integration. Instead of being travelers, we were going to be community members. That integration started with enrolling our kids in school.

Since I'd moved a lot when I was a kid, I knew what first-day jitters felt like for my sons. The feeling I was *not* prepared for was the feeling of knowing that *my* decisions were directly responsible for *their* fear and *their* tears.

Leading through change is like that, isn't it? Even though you believe you're doing the right thing to stretch and strengthen your people, that belief doesn't automatically erase the discomfort.

To make matters worse, I had to give a keynote speech in Miami that first day, so I could only be with them over FaceTime. I couldn't give Rueben and Franklin a hug to assure them everything would be all right. I couldn't wrap my arm around little Lincoln's trembling shoulders and walk him to the door of his kindergarten classroom. Alison and I couldn't be together in person to reassure each other that we weren't permanently damaging our children.

Remember that blissful moment I told you about a few chapters ago—where the clouds parted and the sun shone through at the exact moment Alison and I decided on our shared future dream to spend a year outside the continental United States? What happened next on this day was the exact *opposite* of that moment. Shortly after dropping off her terrified young boys, Alison tearfully stopped at the pharmacy on her way back to our house. While opening the door to get our two-year-old, Gwendolyn, out of her car seat, the sliding van door literally fell off the van and landed on her foot. I have never heard of that happening to anyone's van before or since. Some things you simply can't make up.

Alison spent the rest of the day nursing her foot, regretting our decision, and anxiously waiting for the inevitable phone call from the school telling her that she must immediately pick up her catatonic sons before they went into an irreversible state of traumatic shock due to parental neglect and incompetence—a phone call she wouldn't understand because it would be in Spanish.

After delivering my keynote, I spent the rest of the morning Uber-ing around Miami looking for an auto parts distributor who could supply me with the broken piece of the van door that, for historic-hurricane-related reasons, couldn't be shipped to Puerto Rico by the usual channels for months. The entire time, I had the voice of GOB from *Arrested Development* ringing in my ears: *I've made a huge mistake.*

Finally, the end of the school day came. Alison could finally rescue our little soldiers. And what to her wondering eyes should appear? Three little boys seemingly filled with cheer. They were alive, well, and running around with what appeared to be . . . *friends*! It turns out some kids and teachers had no trouble at all speaking English and were, in fact, eager to use their second language with the newly arrived classmates. As the boys filed back into the van (on the side with the still-functioning door, of course), Alison cautiously asked how school went.

The day that began with tears, terror, and a lingering sense of abandonment ended with a unanimous response of "Best day ever!" Six years later, all four kids are fully bilingual and thriving.

Leading a year of wonders is like that.

MY ORIGIN STORY

I wish I was a little bit taller.
I wish I was a baller.

—Skee-Lo

I first heard about Isaac Newton's year of wonders in April 2020. We were six weeks deep into the COVID-19 pandemic, and my calendar for the rest of the year cleared in a flash . . . along with most of my expected income. That spring was a potent cocktail of worry and wonder. I began to perceive things about my career and my life I'd never noticed before. It was only then, almost thirty years later and in the middle of a global pandemic, that I finally started to rethink a pivotal story from my past. You might even call it my origin story.

The year I turned thirteen years old, my family moved into a different house in a different town four counties, and many Iowa cornfields, away. Although we'd already changed homes six times before, this move came with an added twist. That year I was also diagnosed with a growth hormone deficiency. Essentially, that means one day my pituitary glands took a nap and never woke up. And when your pituitary glands don't produce growth hormone, guess what? You don't grow.

One year away from starting high school, I was four and a half feet tall and barely tipping the scales at sixty-five pounds. You can probably imagine the slack-jawed stares that tracked my steps when I shuffled into my eighth-grade classroom—the New Kid sporting the average height, weight, and soft, round facial features of a second grader. Tall, dark, and handsome, I was not.

As I walked in, I intentionally tilted my chin up in a display of faux confidence and pretended not to notice.

They're probably not looking at me, anyway, I told myself. *Just my nervous mind playing tricks on me. Give 'em a few days, and they'll all want to be my friend.*

Every time I almost had myself convinced this was a much bigger deal in my head than in reality, a kind parent or teacher would stop me in the hall to ask—with well-intentioned sincerity—if they could help me find my way back to the elementary school. Illusion shattered.

But I think what bothered me most was the loss of my identity. I loved playing sports—football, basketball, baseball, wrestling, and swimming. "Athlete" was a big part of who I thought I was back then. Even though I'd always been small compared to other kids my age, in junior high school the size *gap* between me and the other kids widened to a size *chasm*. With every passing month, it seemed the kids around me got twice as big, twice as fast, twice as strong, and twice as coordinated. But I didn't change at all.

The one silver lining was that my condition was so severe that I qualified for a multiyear treatment with synthetic growth hormone. To seize this opportunity, my parents would just have to shell out two-thirds of their annual income every year for the next five years. If mom and dad could do that, and my adolescent self could stick to the plan of sticking my body with a syringe seven days a week, 365 days a year, the doctors assured me that it would only take *three more years* until I might be able to crack the very bottom end of the "normal" size range.

I was sad. I was frustrated. I was worried things were never going to get any better.

But in the midst of all that questioning and confusion, I saw a falling apple. *If my body was struggling to keep up with my peer group, maybe I could change my peer group?*

So, I put on my salesman hat and convinced my parents I should repeat eighth grade. *Wouldn't that give my body another year to catch up with my peers?* I argued. *Because of my summer birthday, and because—not to point fingers—you, my dear parents, jumped the gun when you started me so young in kindergarten, some kids (like my friend Chad) are older than me even though they're a grade behind me.*

My logical argument, balanced with a good measure of guilt-tripping, sold my parents on the plan. I now had hope for a brighter future.

In their infinite wisdom, my parents put one condition on their blessing: run the plan by the school principal before officially pulling the trigger.

Principal Paulsen patiently listened to me plead my

case. Then he looked at my parents. "Nick is a pretty good student, isn't he?" Then he looked at me. "Nick, you like school, don't you?"

I shrugged my shoulders and gave a begrudging nod. Even though I'd never actually said "I like school," my actions betrayed me. Just a few weeks earlier, I'd petitioned Mr. Paulsen to let me join the school's Talented and Gifted program even though I came up a few points short of the IQ cutoff score. Now I was trying to hold myself back.

"I'll support whatever decision you make," Mr. Paulsen said. "But in the long run, in my opinion, it would be a mistake for a solid student to repeat a grade for purely physical reasons." As much as it pained my parents to see one of their kids struggle, they sided with Mr. Paulsen.

Welcome back to the show, Frustration, Confusion, Anger, and Sadness.

Then, right on cue, I saw another falling apple. I thought *If I'm too good at academics to repeat a grade, maybe I can find some scholarly pursuits to satisfy my competitive drive?* I knew the school spelling bee was coming up. And since size doesn't help you spell, I decided to participate.

And what do you know? I won.

Something about being up on stage in front of all my classmates sparked another falling apple: even though I was struggling in sports, I was succeeding at making friends. I think the other kids were surprised and delighted that somebody so little and cute and doughy could also be kind of smart and kind of funny. The other kids really were looking at me, and that preoccupation with my unique stature could be an advantage. Ursula Burns—former CEO of Xerox and the first Black female CEO of a Fortune 500 company—described a similar revelation she had during her climb up the corporate ladder: "If you're one or two of forty or fifty, you're a freak show. . . . So if I raised my hand, I was always called on, because, I mean, you couldn't miss me."* Like Burns, I discovered that what I viewed as an obstacle to overcome was also an opportunity I could exploit.

I decided to parlay the other kids' social curiosity into support for my bid to become the next year's class president. Believe it or not, I won that too.

For decades, I chalked up that year's successes to nothing more than a cosmic consolation prize. I had convinced myself those little wins were simply the universe's way of saying, "Sorry for the dumpster fire, kid. Here's a three-dollar spelling bee trophy." I saw myself as the protagonist of a classic underdog story—a victim of fate whose never-surrender attitude overcame impossibly long odds. *Yay for me!*

But my discovery during the pandemic of Newton's year of wonders was a falling apple for me. Only then, during that period of change, pressure, and uncertainty, did I recognize that the story I'd been telling myself about my childhood was tragically incomplete. I finally saw that what I'd always thought of as a change-filled

---

* From an interview by Adi Ignatius, "I'm Here Because I'm as Good as You," published in *Harvard Business Review*, July/August 2021.

year of worry with a few token victories was actually an insight-filled year of wonders capped off by big wins that laid the foundation for my future calling as a writer and a speaker.

Although the pandemic was still a long way from over and I was still worried, I also began to wonder. I wondered what insights I was going to have. I wondered what skills I was going to develop. I wondered what stories I would be able to tell. I wondered if this experience would somehow help me change the way you and the people around you think about change.

This book is the result of those wonders. I hope in some small way it has been a falling apple for you.

ABOUT THE AUTHOR

Nick Tasler is an organizational psychologist and a globally recognized expert on the science of embracing change. He has helped hundreds of thousands of leaders around the world transform seasons of change into periods of unprecedented growth at the world's most respected organizations ranging from FedEx, Microsoft, and JPMorgan Chase to Walmart, Yale University, and more.

Nick has been a leadership columnist at the *Harvard Business Review* and a guest lecturer at the Wharton School, and his ideas have been featured by the *New York Times*, *Fast Company*, NPR, Fox News, the BBC, and leading media outlets around the world.

Nick and his wife and their four kids live in Puerto Rico.